Merry Christmas

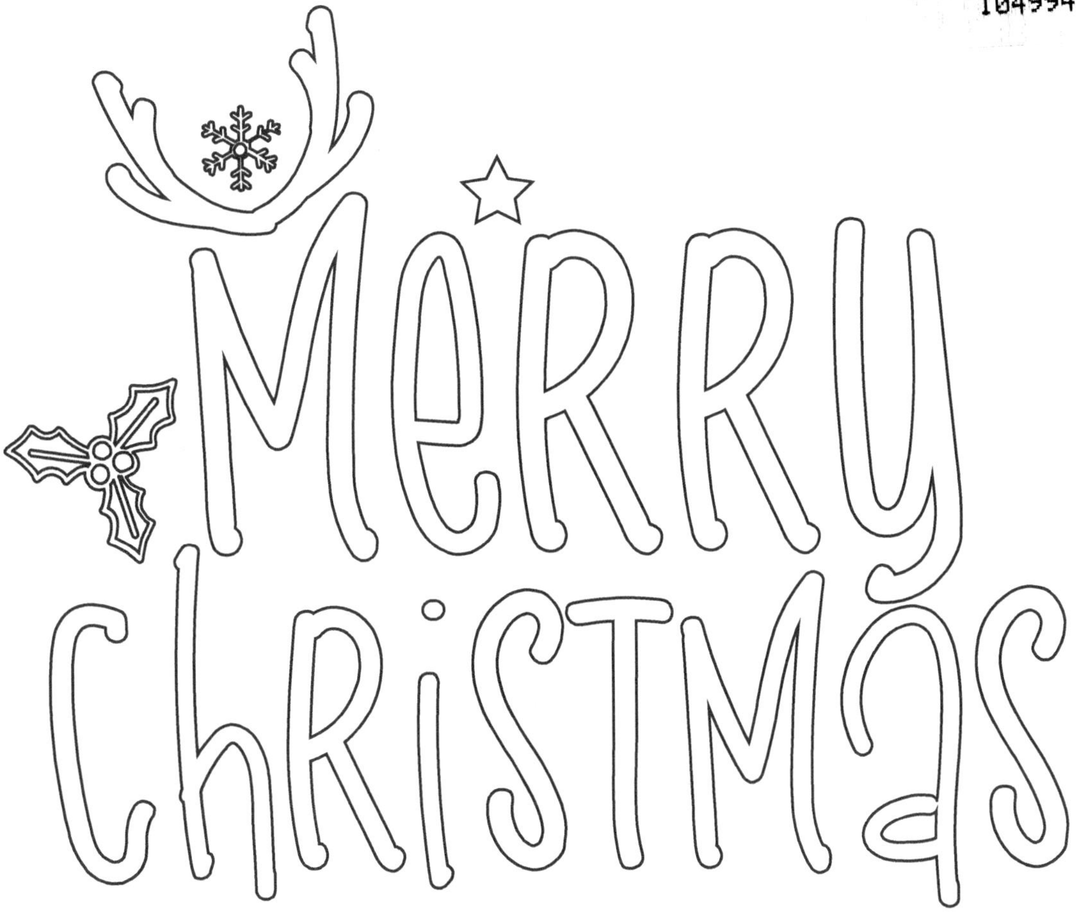

This Book Belongs To:

_____

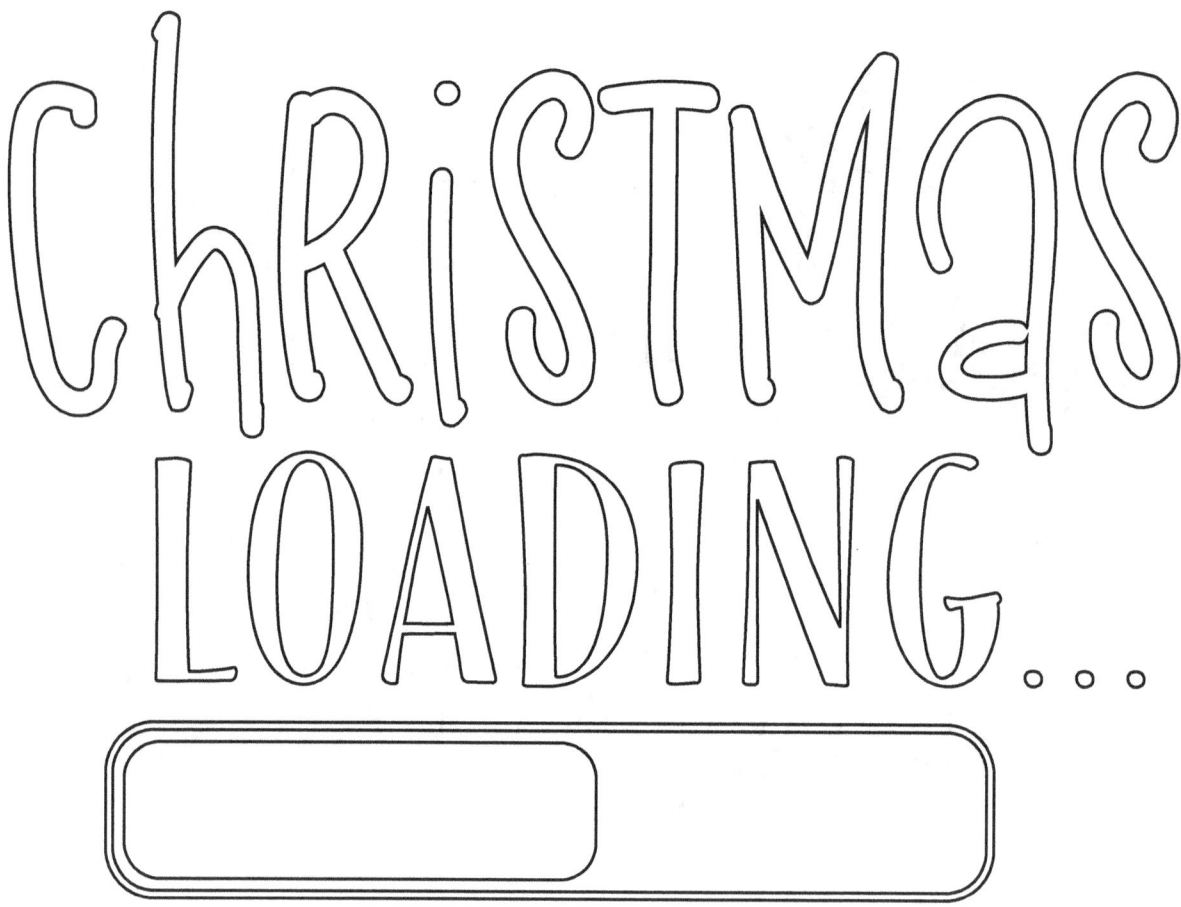

© 2019 Practical Journals and Planners
All rights reserved. No part of this book may be reproduced
or transmitted in any form or by any means electronical
or mechanical including photocopying, recording, scanning
or any other information storage retrieval system
without permission from the Publisher.

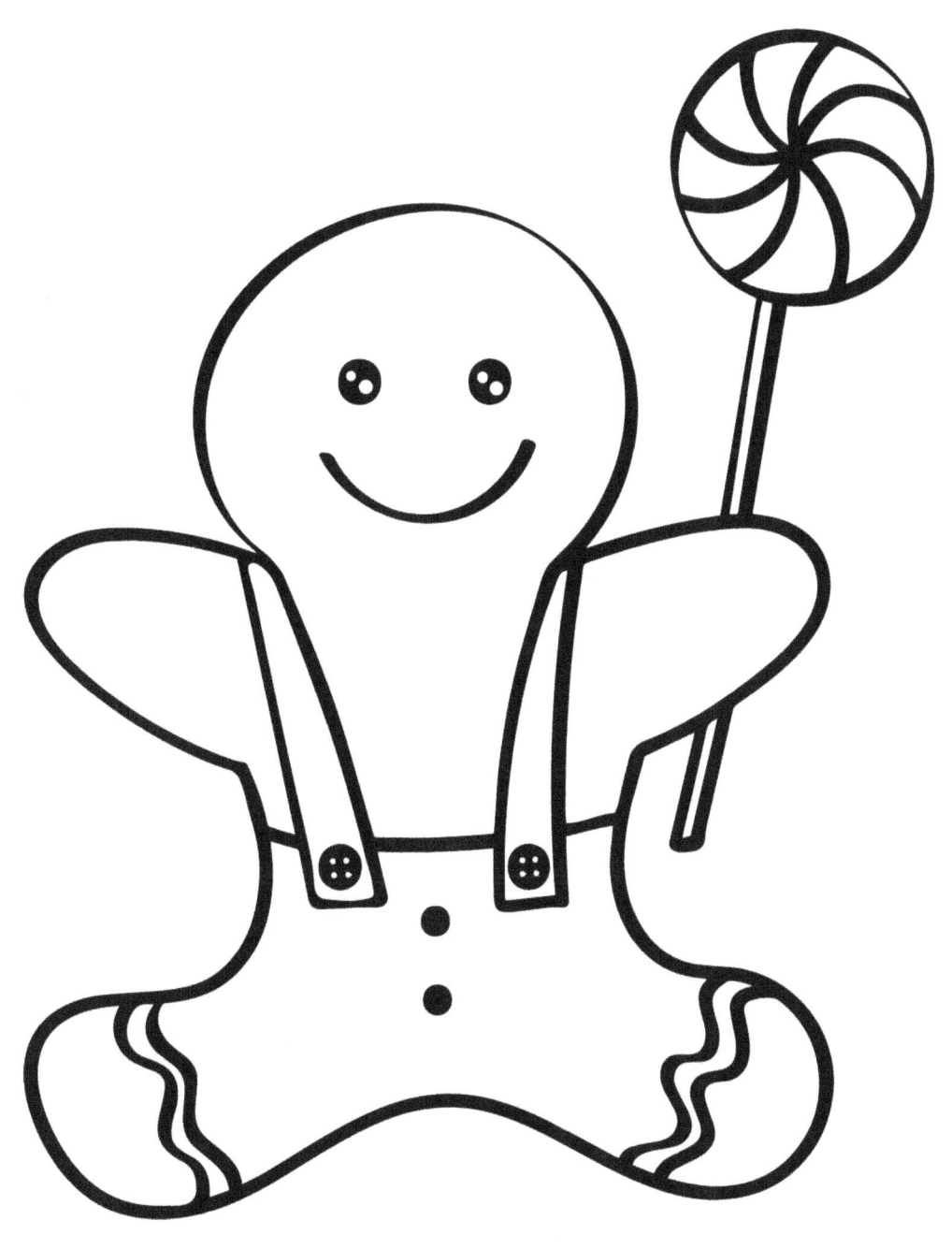

Believe

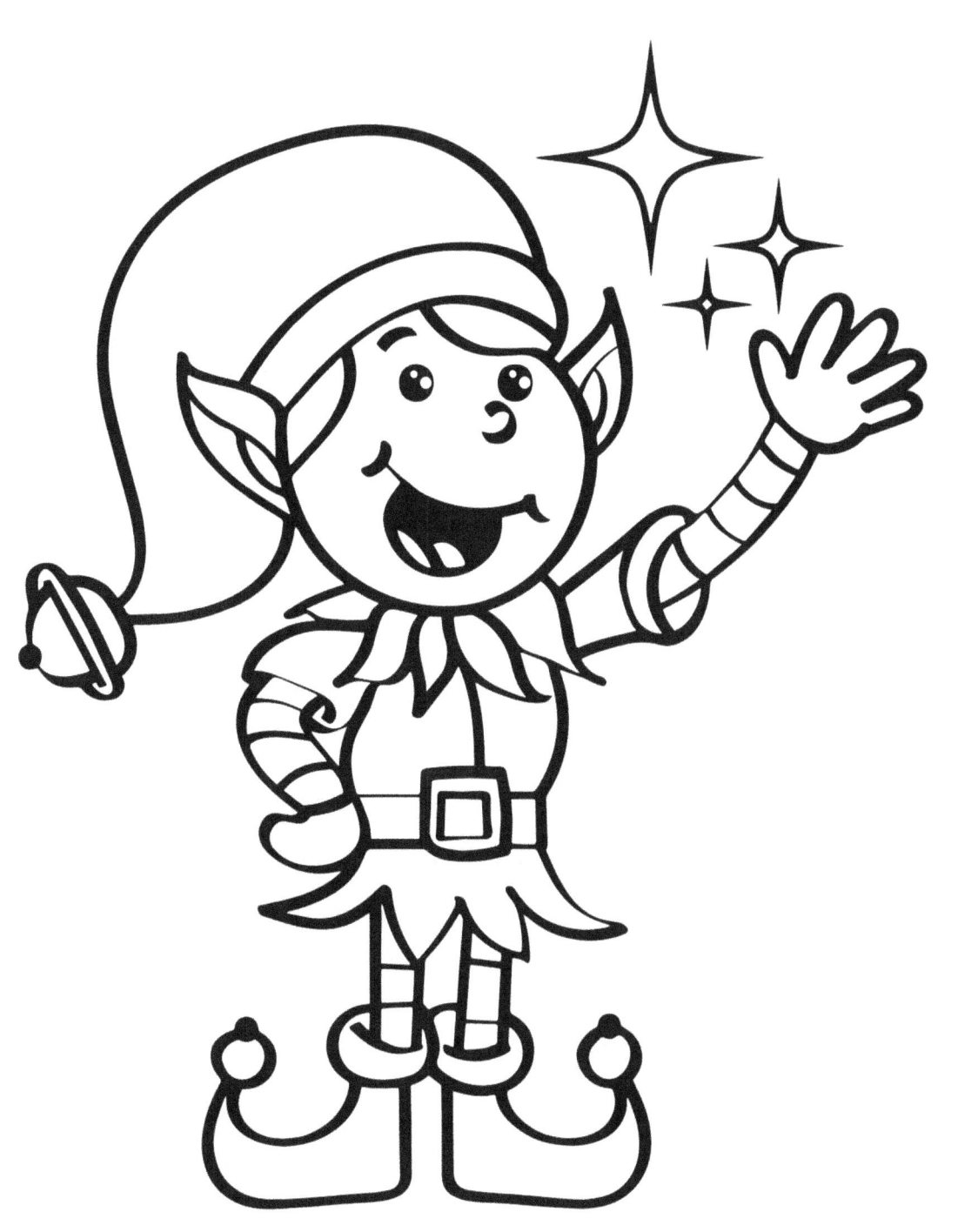

CANDY CANE CUTIE

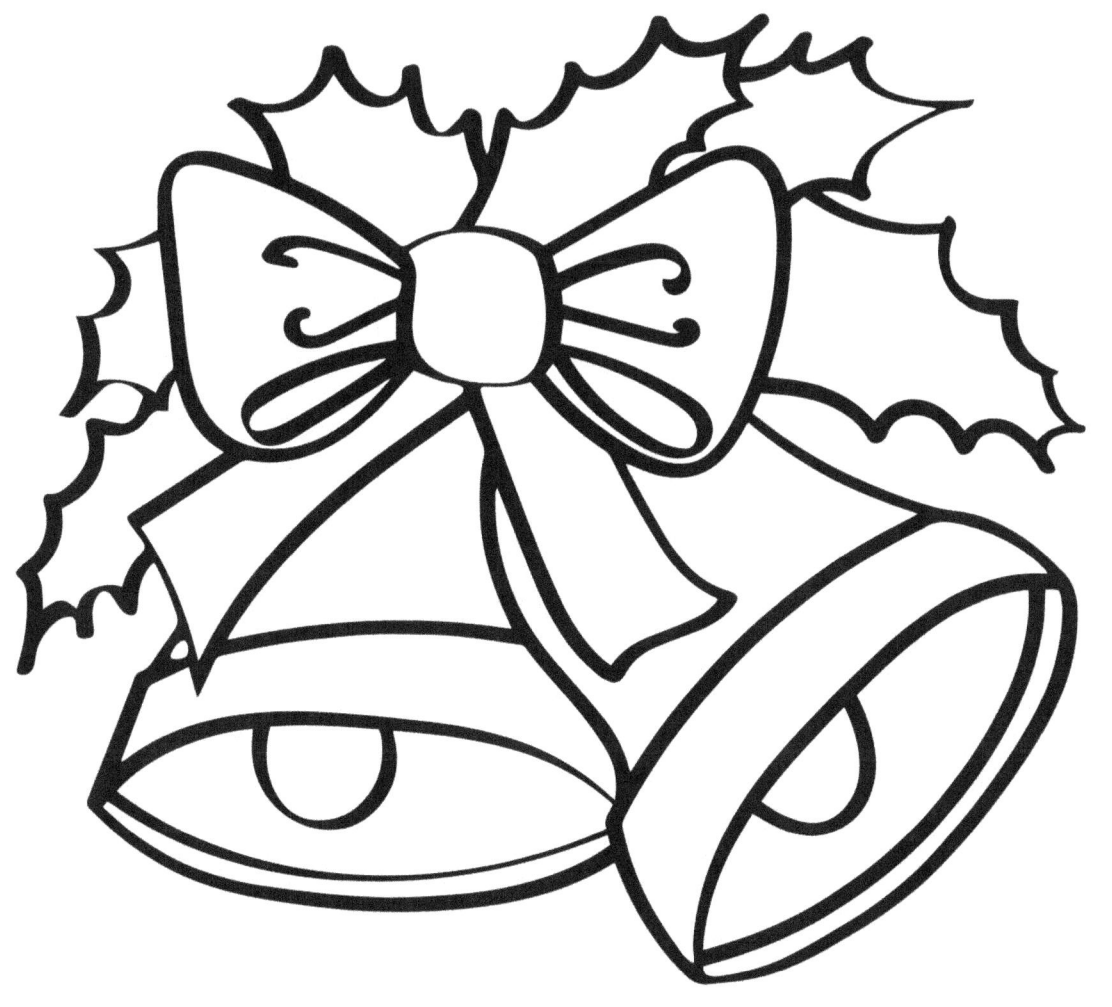

DEAR SANTA DEFINE GOOD

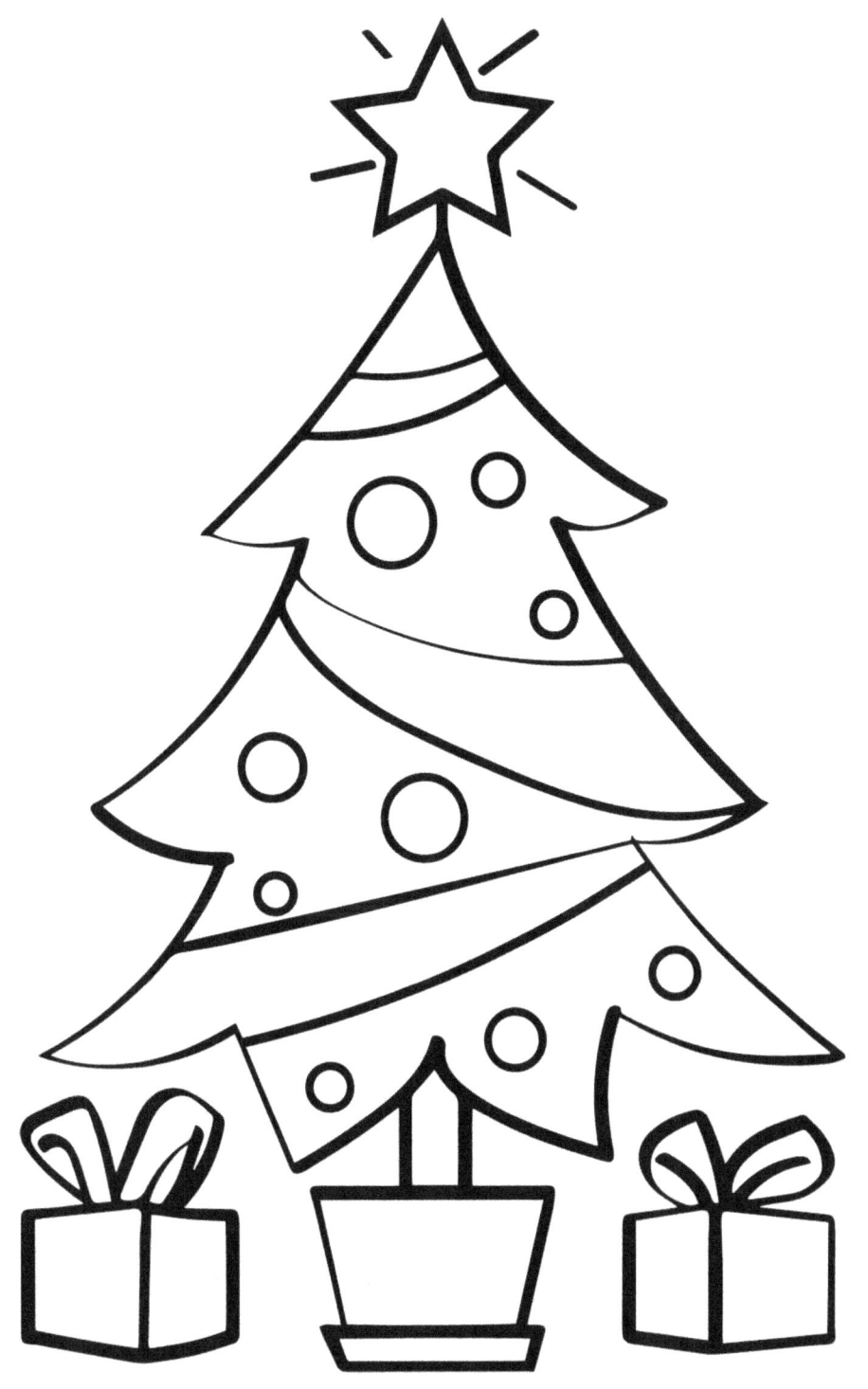

COOKIES FOR SANTA

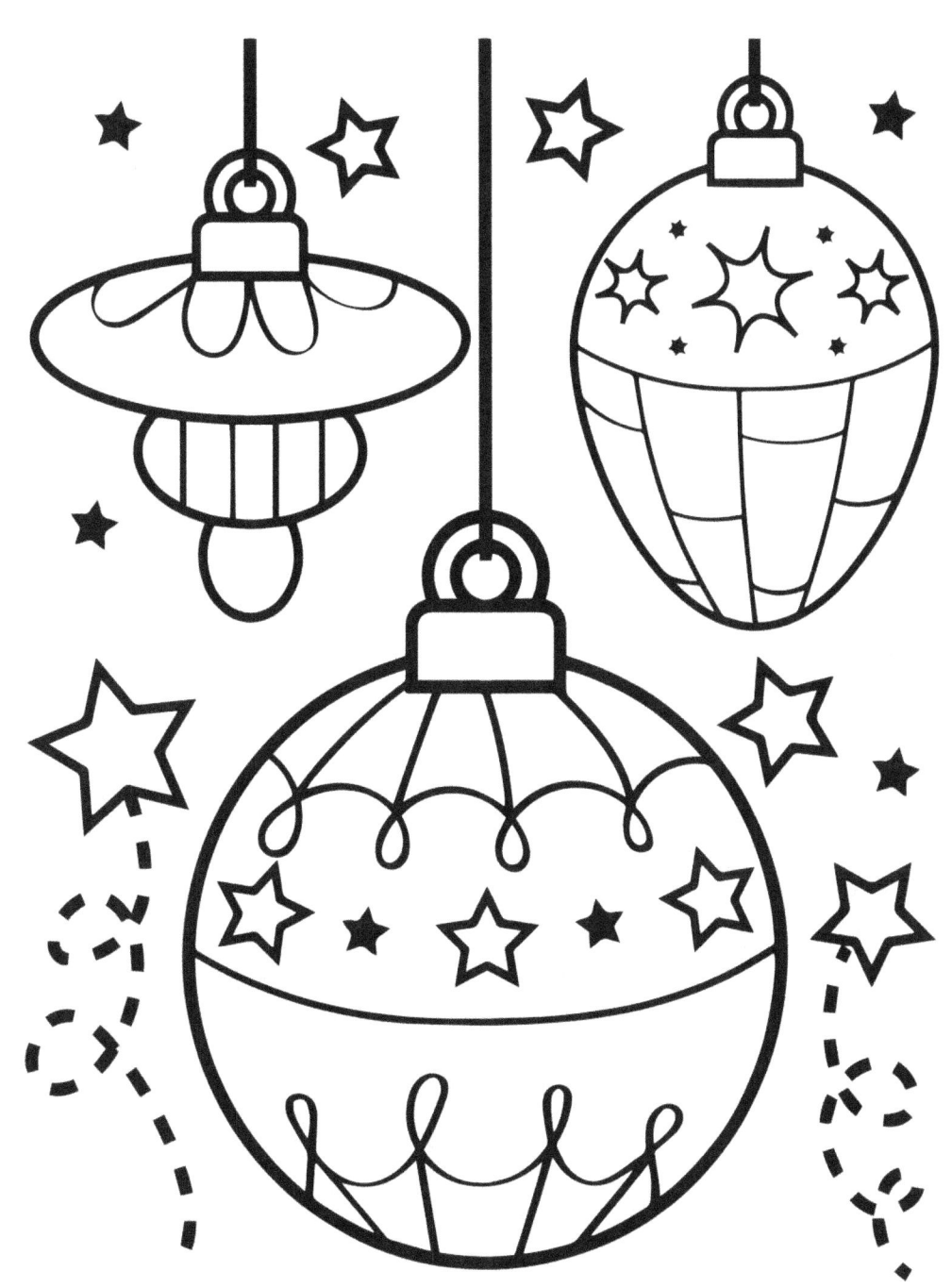

CARROTS FOR THE REINDEER

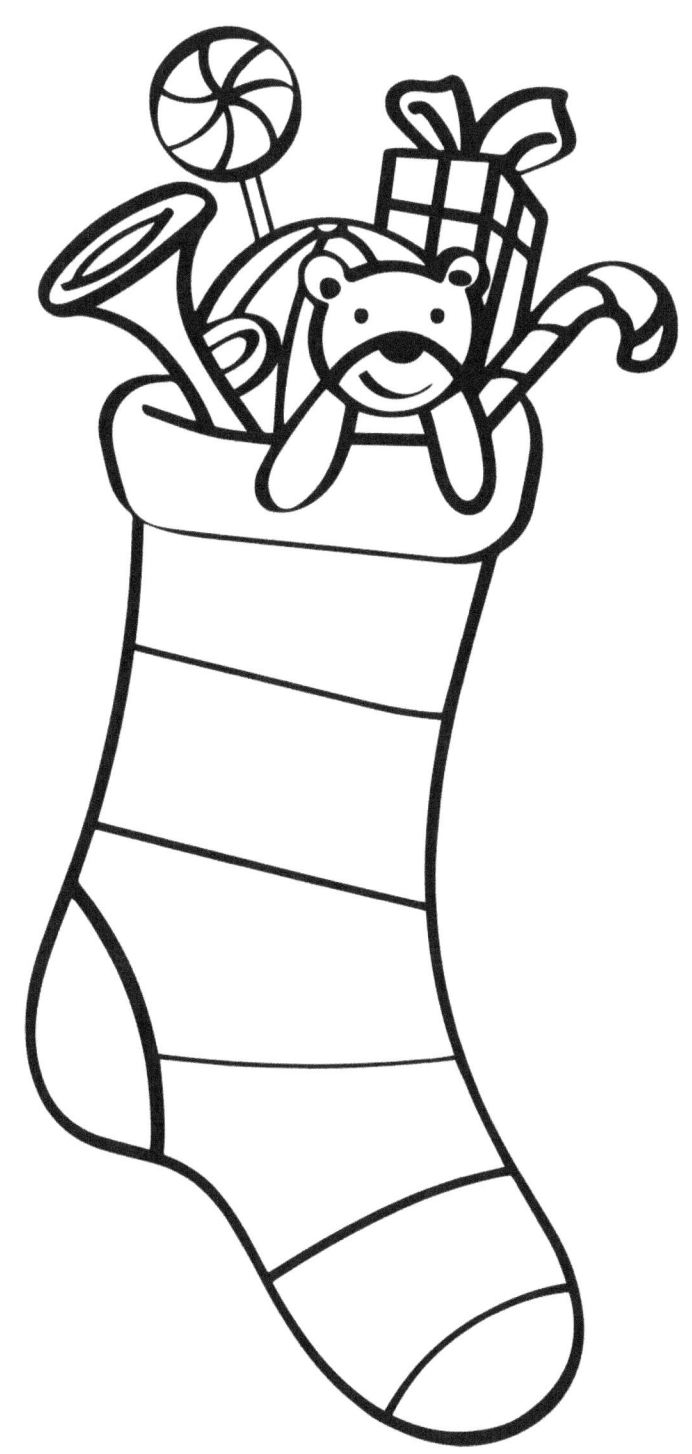

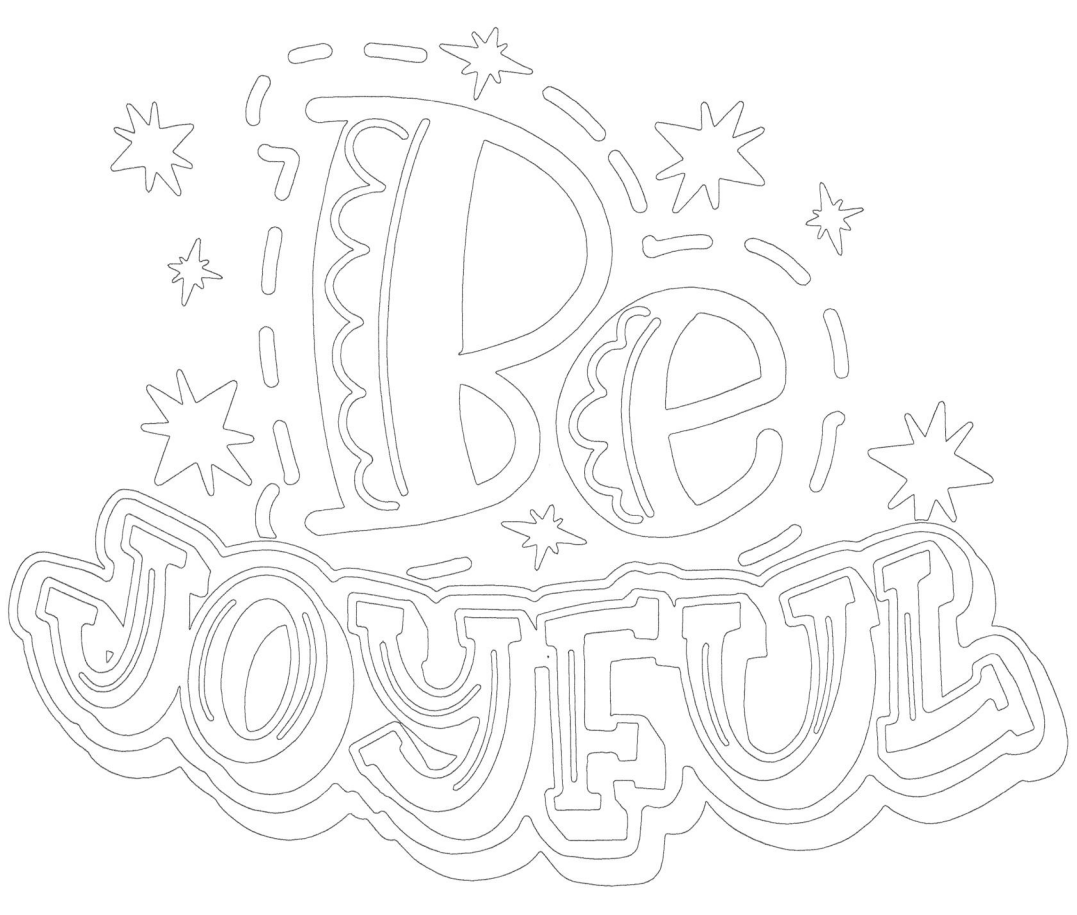

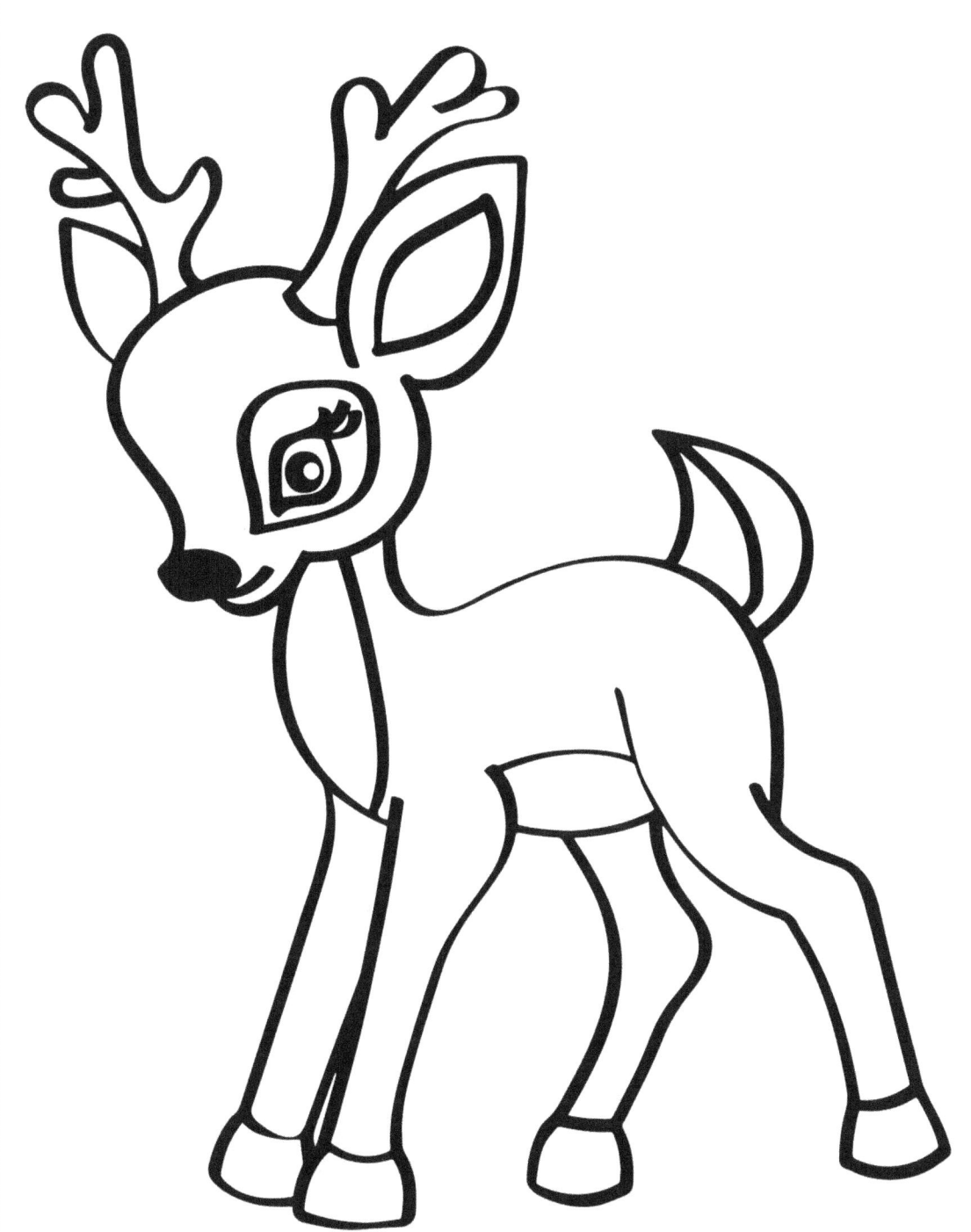

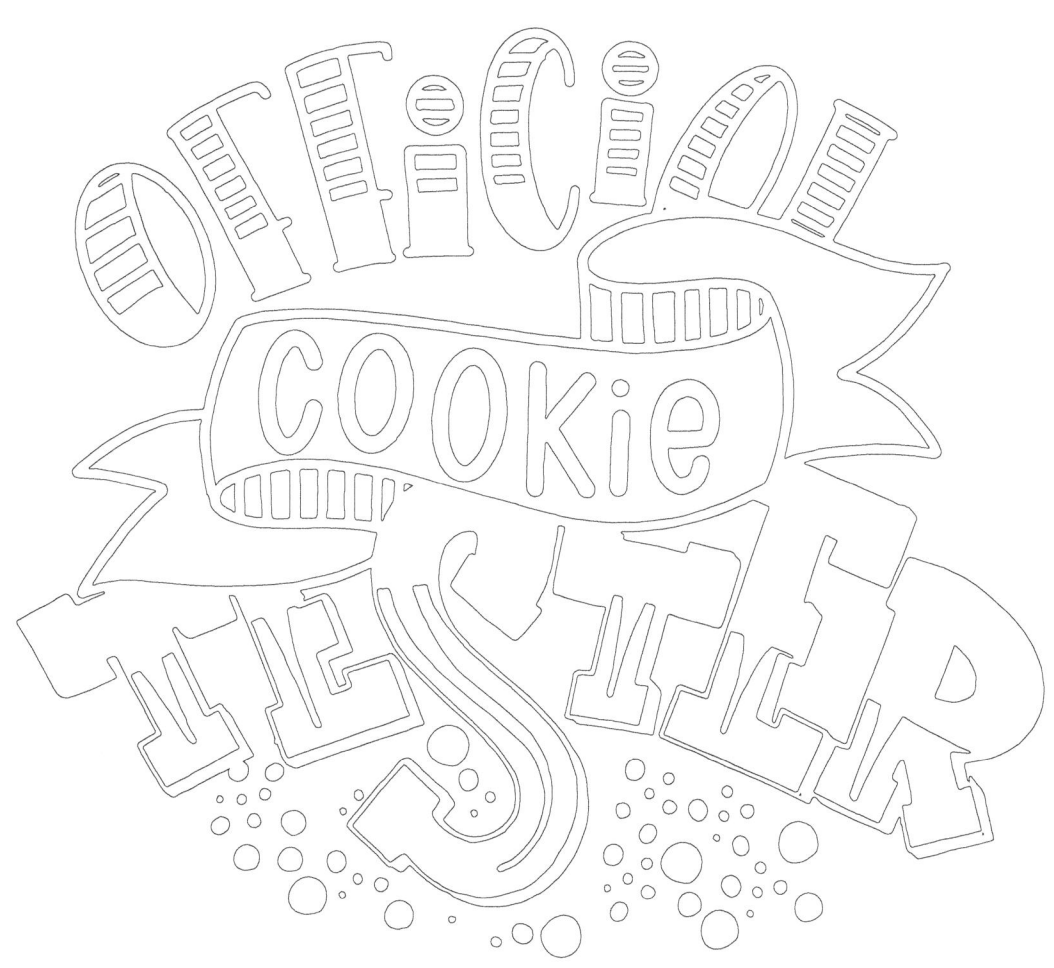

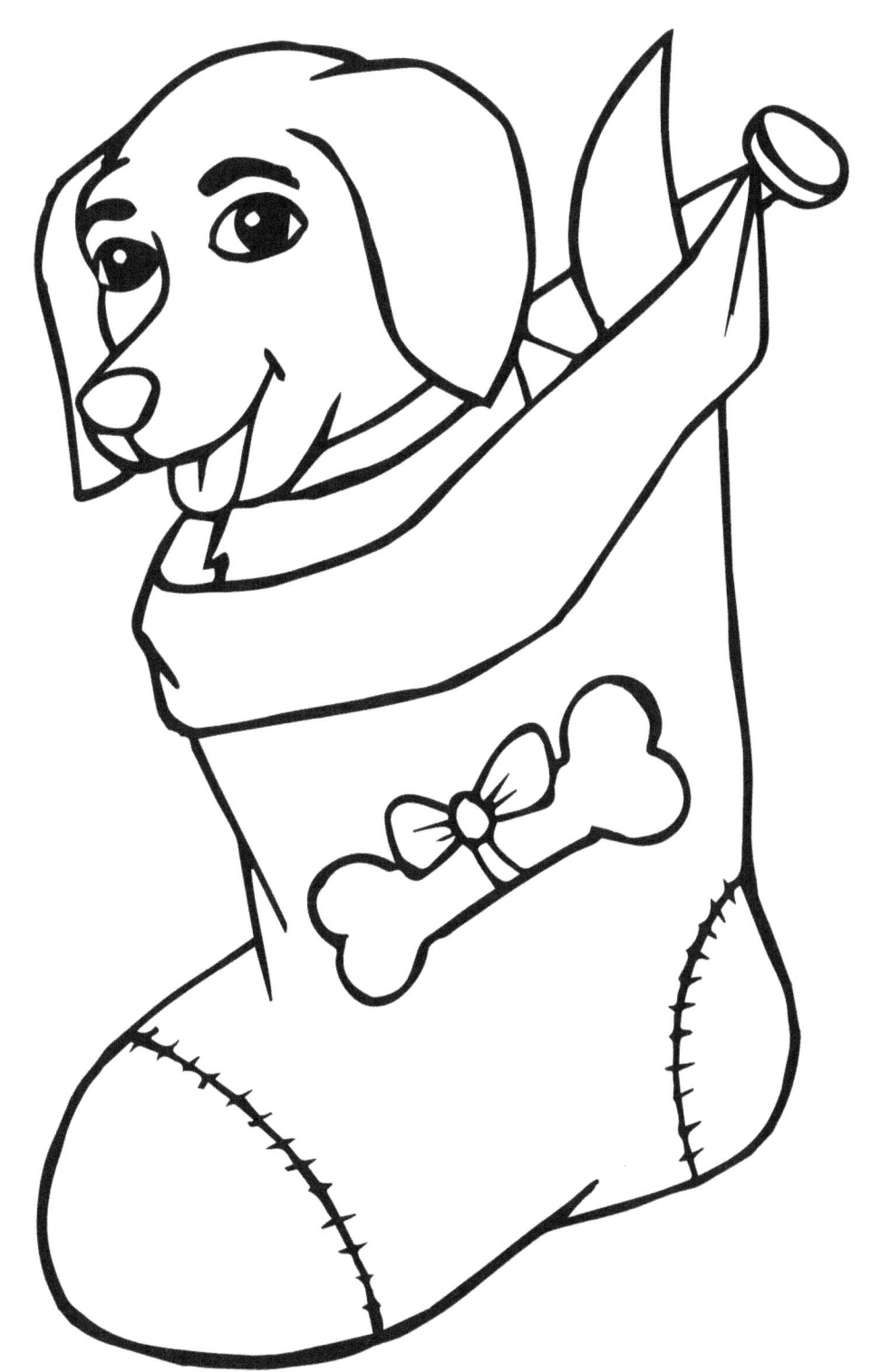

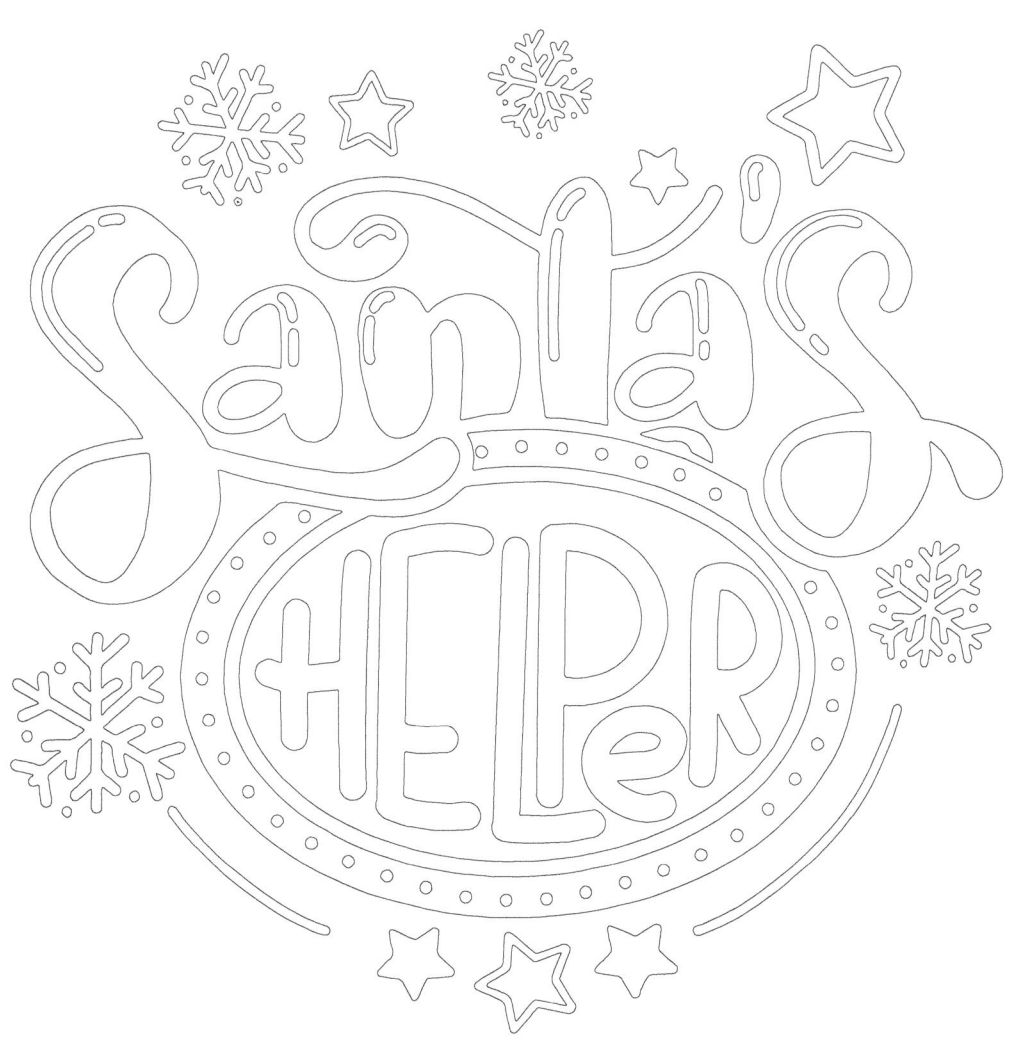

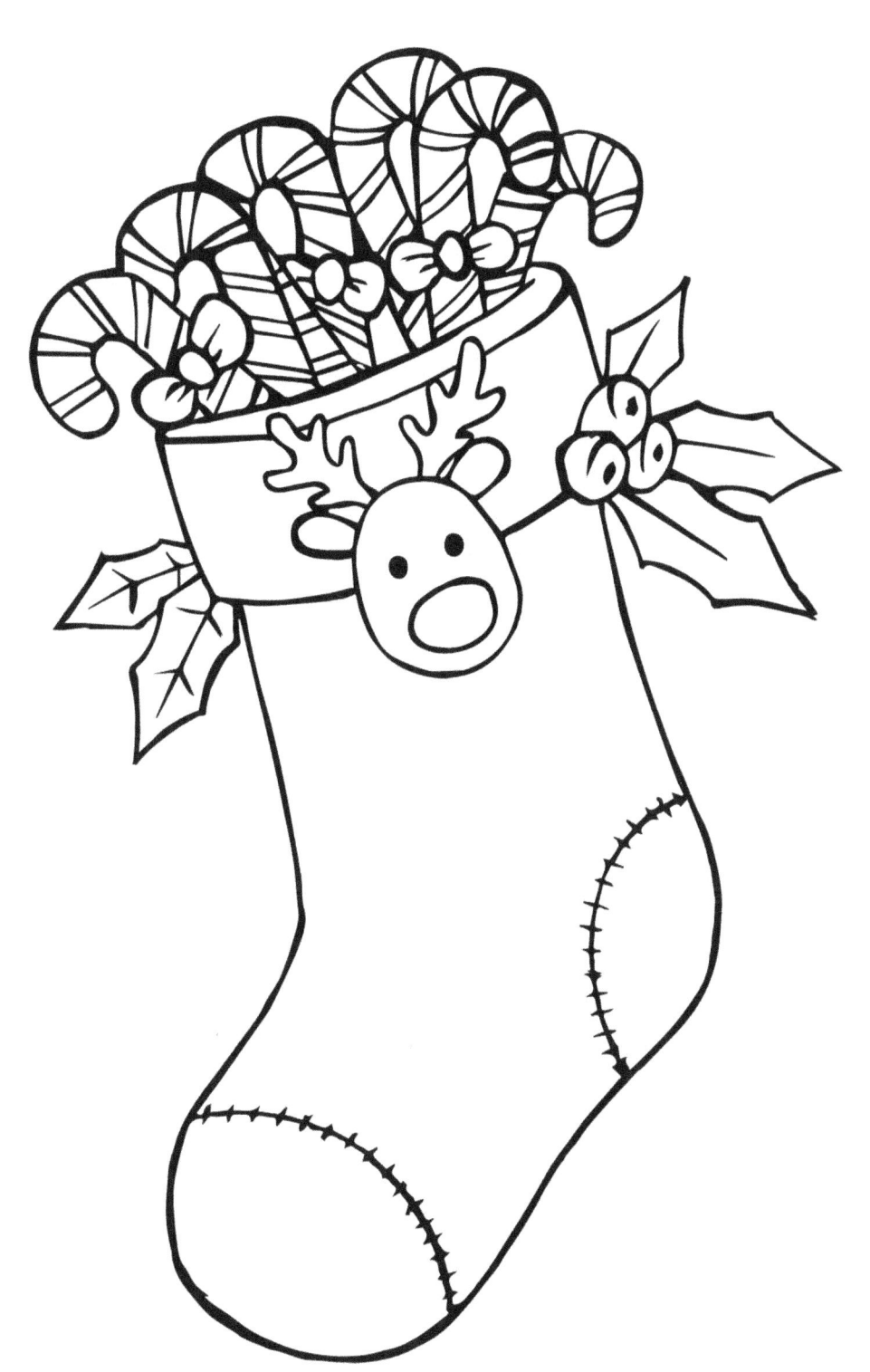

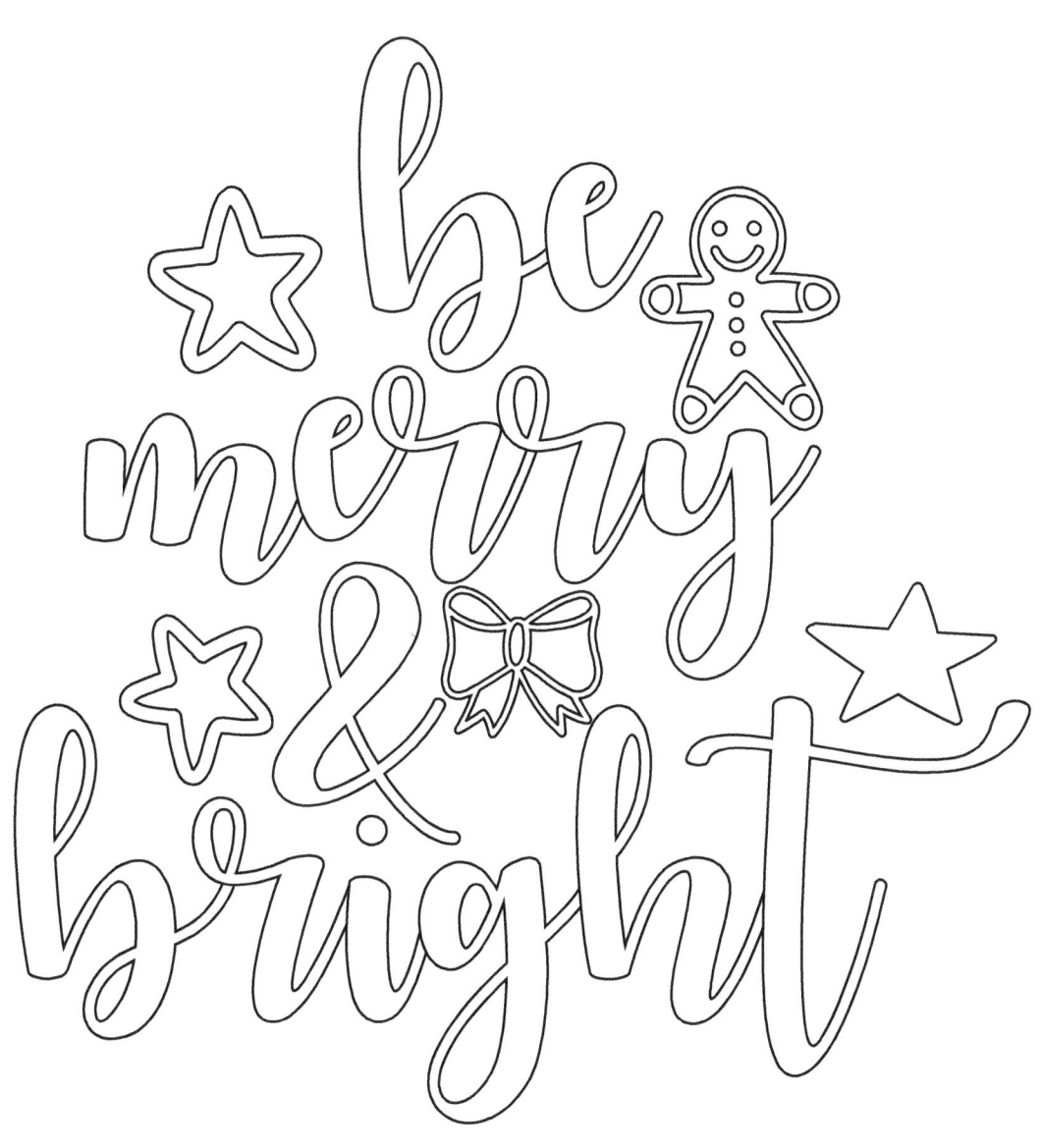

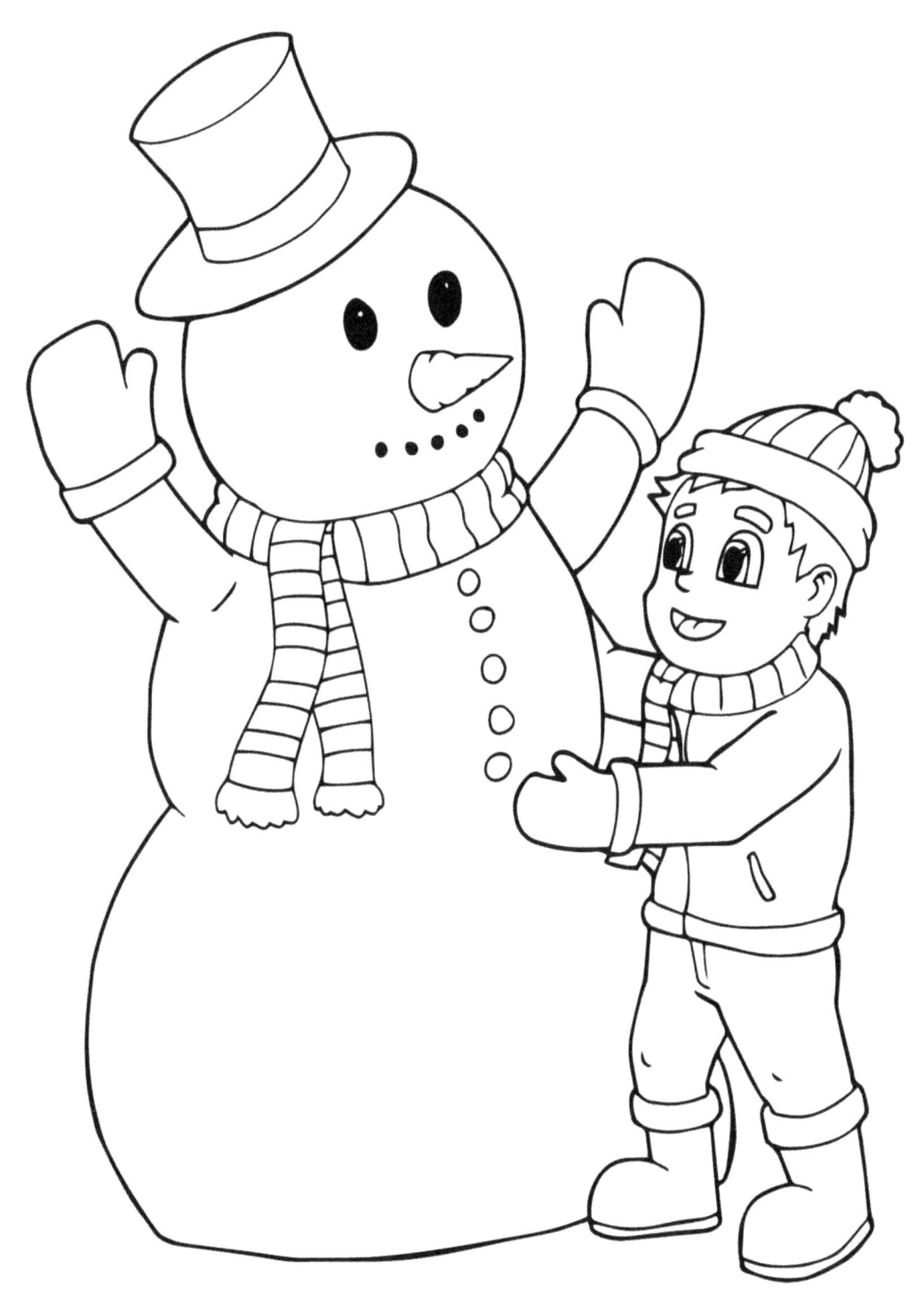

tis the season to be jolly

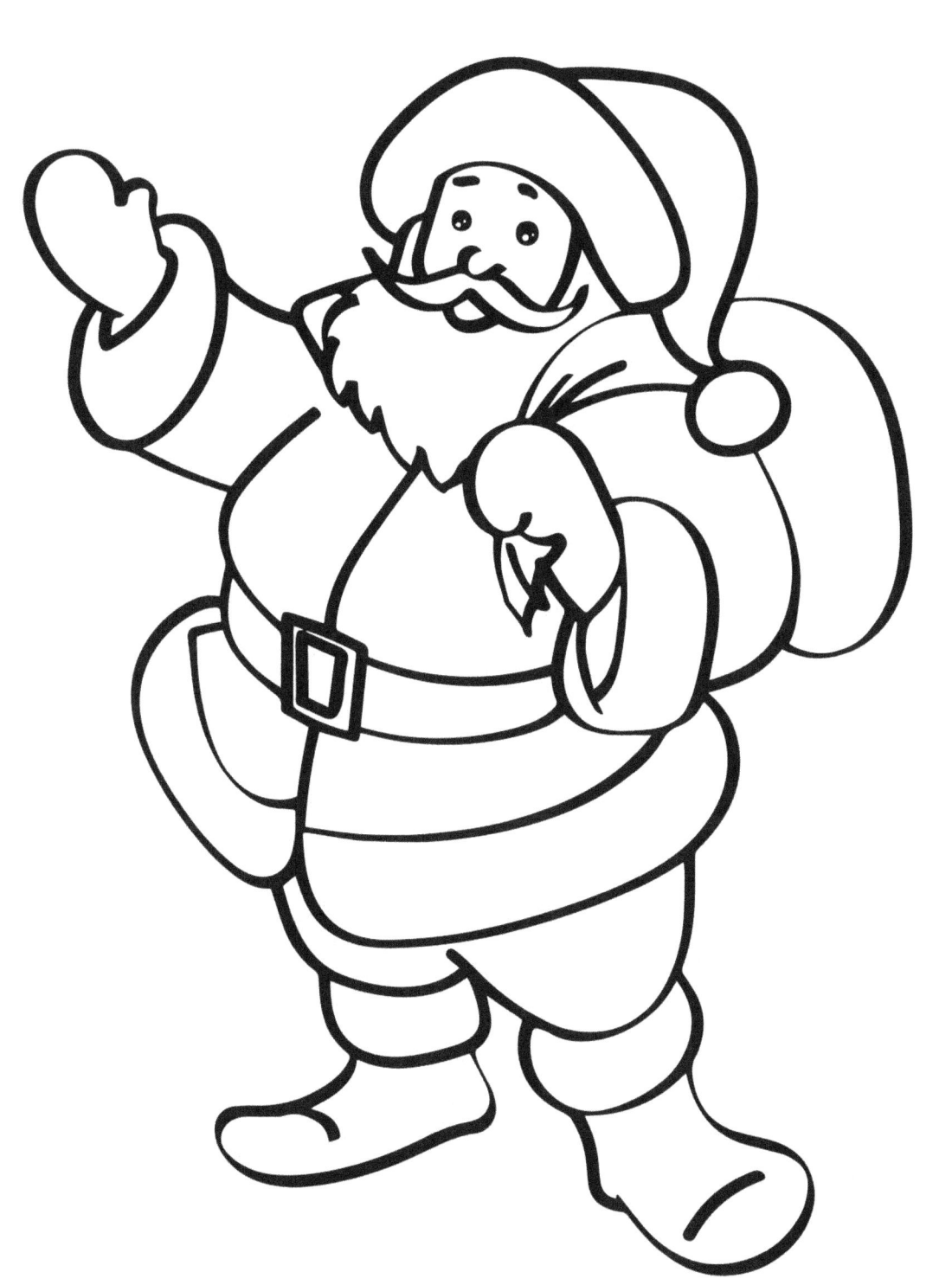

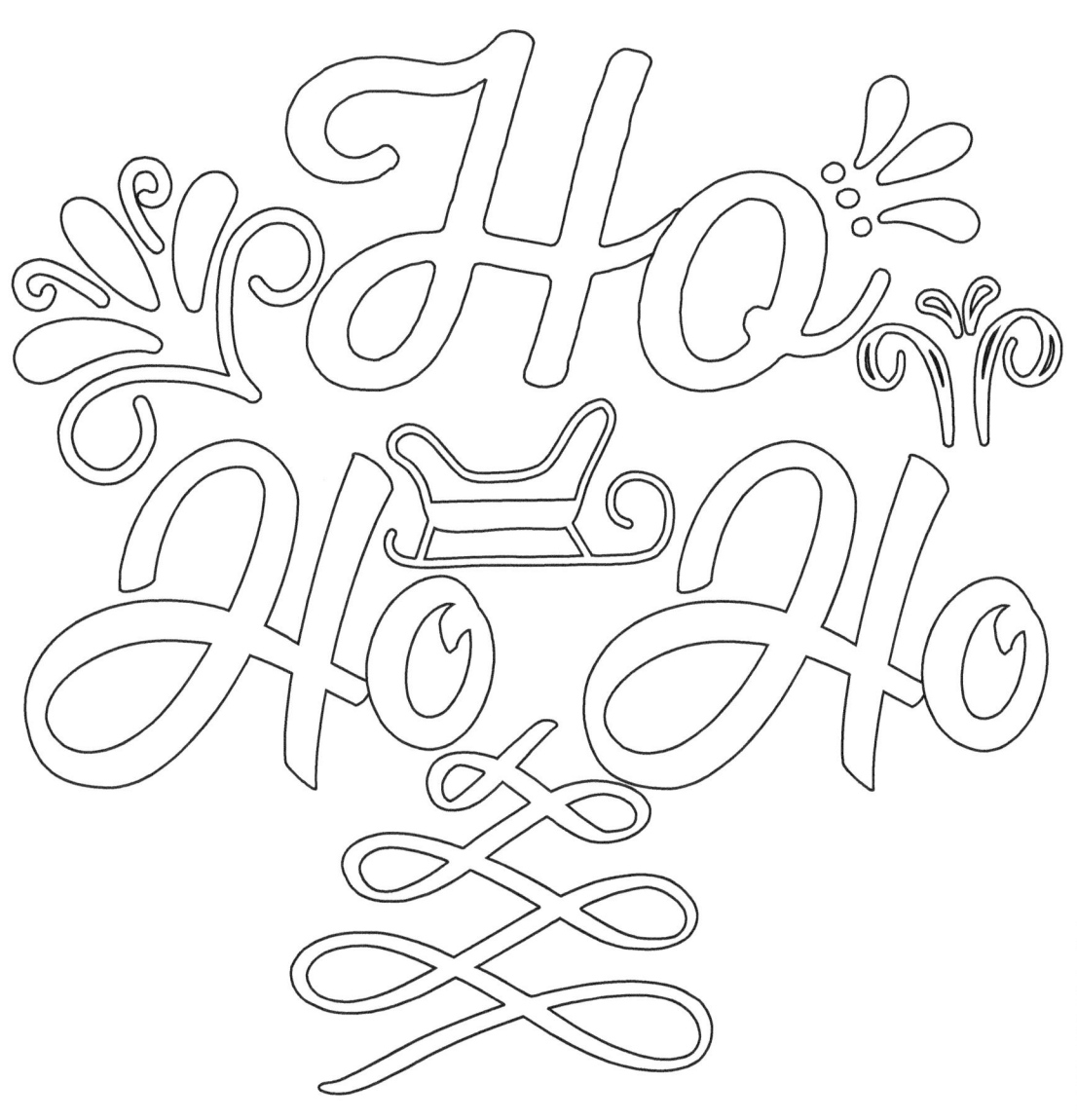

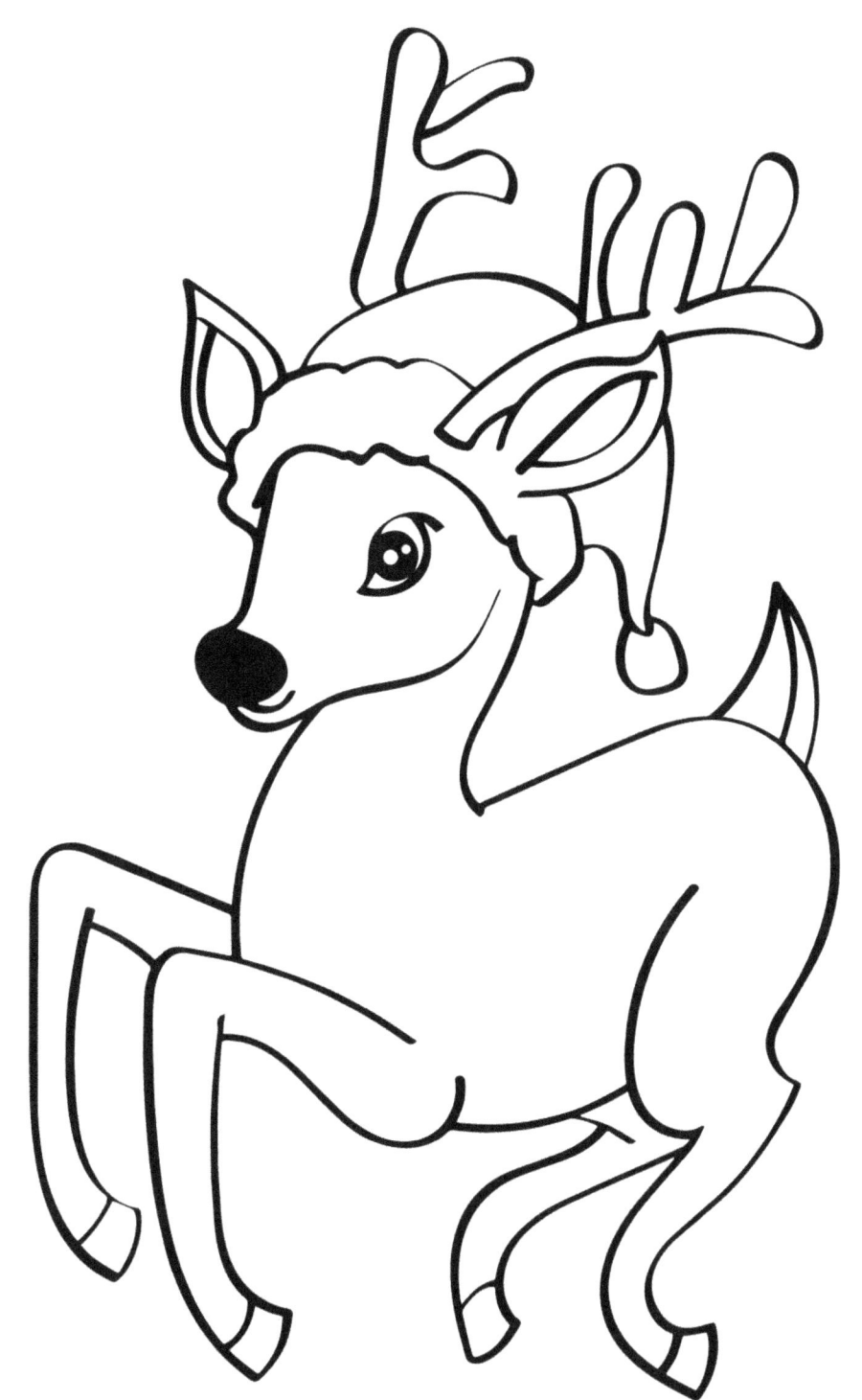

Dear Santa I can explain

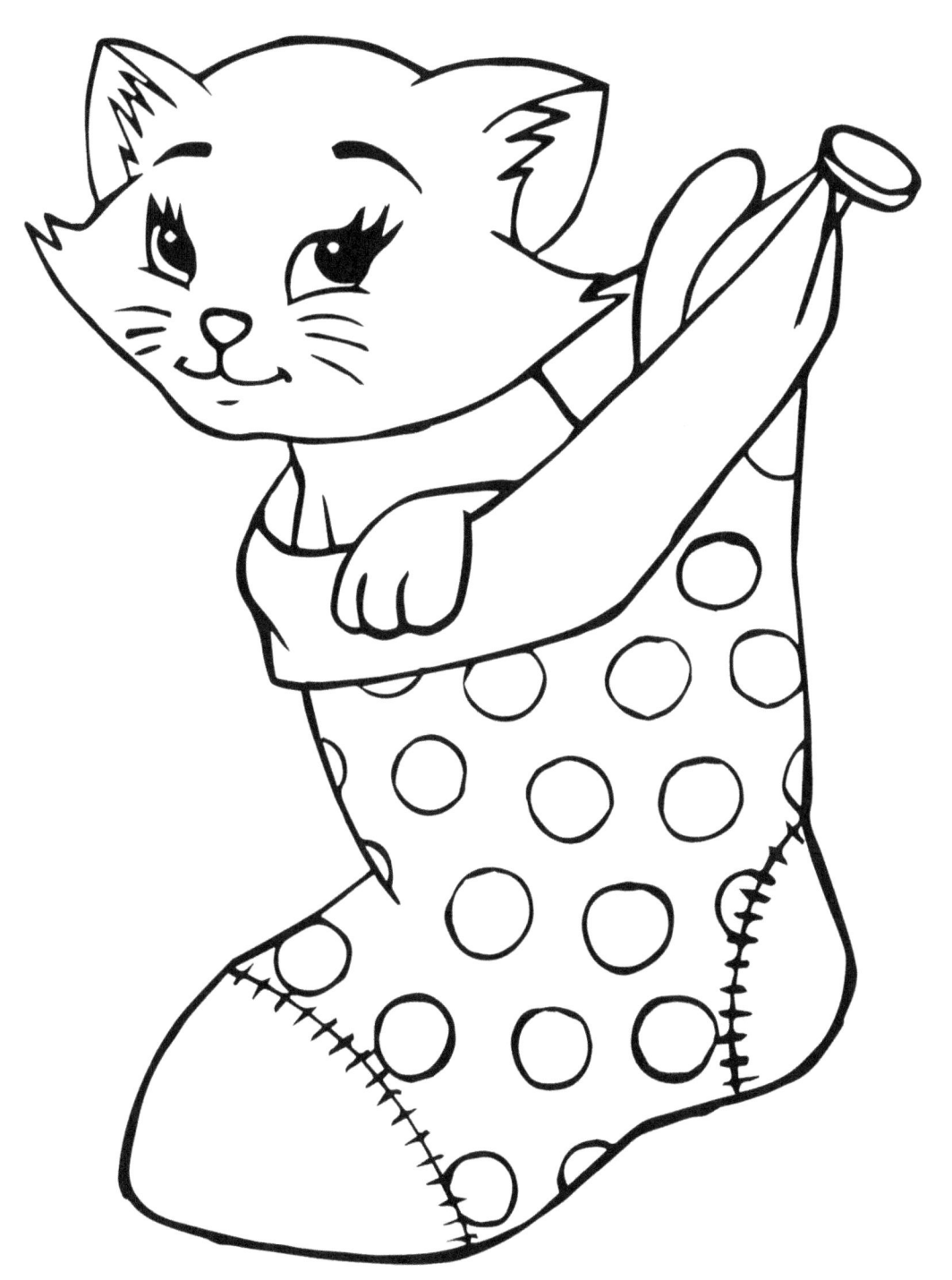

www.ingramcontent.com/pod-product-compliance
Lightning Source LLC
Chambersburg PA
CBHW081658220526
45466CB00009B/2809